# IN THIS SERIES

Geo. Morris.

W. Dunn.

David Park.

Tom Morris, Jun.

A. Strath.

Bob Kirk.

W. Dow.

Jas. Ande

Jas. Dunn.

Alexr. Greig.

Tom Morris.

# GRAND GOLF TOURNAMENT BY PROFESSIONAL PLAYERS

*On Leith Links, 17th May, 1867.*

*THE COMPOSITE GUIDE*

## to **GOLF**

**MARY E. HULL**

**CHELSEA HOUSE PUBLISHERS**

Philadelphia

**Produced by Choptank Syndicate, Inc.**

Editor and Picture Researcher: Norman L. Macht
Production Coordinator and Editorial Assistant: Mary E. Hull
Design and Production: Lisa Hochstein
Cover Illustrator: Cliff Spohn
Cover Design: Keith Trego
Art Direction: Sara Davis

Cover Design: Keith Trego
Art Direction: Sara Davis

First Printing

1 3 5 7 9 8 6 4 2

Library of Congress Cataloging-in-Publication Data

Hull, Mary
        The composite guide to golf / Mary E. Hull.
            p.  cm.—(The composite guide)
        Includes bibliographical references (p.  ) and index.
        Summary: Traces the story of golf, from its beginnings, to its first stars
    and championship games, to the notable players of today.
        ISBN 0-7910-4726-1
        1. Golf—History—Juvenile literature.          [1. Golf.]          I. Title.
    II. Series.
    GV963.H85       1997
    796.352—dc21                                                    97-30644
                                                                         CIP
                                                                         AC

# CONTENTS

# 1 SETTING GOLF ON FIRE

**A**s Tiger Woods teed off at the 1997 Masters Tournament on April 10, one of the largest galleries ever assembled at Augusta National crowded near the first tee. Woods's reputation as the most talented young man in golf preceded him, and the crowd had come to see the phenom in his first Masters. Woods started out with a four-over-par on the front 9, but settled down to shoot 30 on the back 9, ending the first day with a round of 70 and a place on the leaderboard. Friday's 65 and Saturday's 66 earned him the largest 54-hole lead in the history of the Masters. It was the first of many Masters records Tiger would make or break. On Sunday, knowing that he needed a 69 or better to beat the tournament's 72-hole record of 18 under par, Tiger shot a 69 and won his first major as a professional with a record 270. He became the youngest golfer ever to win the Masters, and his lead of 12 shots over runner-up Tom Kite set another record. Tiger Woods was also the first player widely identified as African-American (Woods is actually of Thai, Chinese, Cherokee, Caucasian, and African-American heritage) to win the Masters Tournament, which had maintained a "Caucasians only" law until 1961 and did not invite a black player until 1975.

The hundreds of black spectators in the crowd that followed Woods around the course included Atlanta Hawks guard Mookie Blaylock,

*1996 Masters Champion Nick Faldo helps Tiger Woods into the coveted green jacket following his record-breaking victory at the 1997 Masters Tournament. Woods set a new record for the lowest score (270), won by the greatest margin of victory ever (12 strokes), and became the youngest person, at 21, to ever win the Masters.*

who "did everything I could to see this young man play golf. It was something I couldn't miss." Woods did not disappoint his fans. His performance gave the Masters its highest television ratings in history. Many people who had never before watched a golf match tuned in to see Tiger play. NBC Sports executive producer Tommy Roy remarked, "He is something that golf hasn't seen since Arnold Palmer. He has tons of charisma, and a heck of a golf game to match. Tiger is attracting the general sports fan, not just the golf fan."

Watching Woods play, wrote columnist George Will, is "like watching Babe Ruth in the 1920s." Woods's skill and his ability to play successfully under pressure have also invited comparisons to Jack Nicklaus. According to Masters runner-up Tom Kite, Woods "has a [swing] speed differential that no one else has had since Jack [Nicklaus] came along in the 1960s. He's leapfrogged everyone in terms of distance." With his long, accurate drives of up to 350 yards, Woods was able to shrink the links and play Augusta as though it were a much easier course. As his adversaries have noted, Woods is, on the golf course, much older than 21.

Woods proved that despite his youth, he had what it takes to play under pressure and compete with the big names. And his success brought a new interest in golf—call it "Tigermania"—especially among young adults who had never played. Woods changed the scene of professional golf with his youth, talent, and background. The effects of his popularity compared to that of another young man, one who rocked the golf world in 1913 and proved that golf was not just a wealthy gentleman's game.

At the beginning of the 20th century Francis Ouimet did for golf what Woods did for the sport at the close of the century. But, unlike the hoopla surrounding Tiger, no one was watching when Ouimet teed off at the beginning of the 1913 U.S. Open. All eyes were on the famous players, the British giants of golf, Harry Vardon and Ted Ray, who had just toured the country, winning every American championship they entered except one. Vardon and Ray were expected to vie for the U.S. Open title, and America had all but given up hope of hanging on to its silver trophy. But a 20-year-old amateur whom the USGA officials had rounded up to help fill out the field changed all that.

Francis Ouimet had grown up playing golf on a homemade course behind his parents' house in Brookline, Massachusetts, which was across the street from the posh country club where the U.S. Open was being held that year. Ouimet had a job in a local sporting goods store, but he caddied at the club just so he could have a chance to play a few holes in the early morning hours before his loop (his caddying job) began. An amateur golfer, Ouimet had tried to qualify for the U.S. Amateur three years in a row, and all three times he was shut out. On his fourth try, he qualified but played poorly in the tournament. Ouimet was not expecting to excel in the Open; he only hoped to catch sight of Vardon or Ray doing their thing. But by the end of the third round on the rainy first day, Ouimet, as much to his surprise as everyone else's, was tied

*An elated Francis Ouimet, ex-caddie of the country club, is carried on the shoulders of fans after his upstart victory over British golf giants Harry Vardon and Ted Ray at the 1913 U.S. Open held in Brookline, Massachusetts.*

with the champions for the lead. When Vardon and Ray finished the fourth round, both with 79s, Ouimet thought he had a chance to beat them. But on the tenth hole, he botched his drive and had to putt three times. Then he bogeyed the twelfth hole. Now, just to tie Vardon and Ray, he had to play the last six holes in two under par. In an amazing display of skill under pressure, the young Ouimet did just that.

The three-way tie forced a playoff the next day in the pouring rain. Vardon and Ray played poorly, rattled by the young upstart. Vardon shot a 77 and Ray a 78, while Ouimet managed a 72. The victory of an unknown American kid over the greatest reigning champions of golf brought the sport to the front pages of American newspapers. Ouimet was a humble winner: "Naturally, it was my hope to win out," he said to the crowd. "I simply tried my best to keep this cup from going to our friends across the water. I am very glad to have been the agency for keeping the cup in America."

Ouimet's victory altered the face of golf. The stereotypes of golf in America in 1913 were that only wealthy men played at exclusive clubs, and the best players in the game were British. Ouimet showed the world that it wasn't so. His triumph created unprecedented interest in the sport. In 1913 there were 350,000 American golfers, but by 1923, over 2 million Americans were playing golf. The game that had begun centuries ago in Europe had finally caught on in America.

# 2

# THE BEGINNINGS OF THE GAME

It is said that the game of golf began when people first saw the fun in hitting small stones into holes with clubs or sticks. Scotland is considered the birthplace of golf as we know the game today. Seaside grasslands, along with paths cleared by rabbits, foxes, and hunters, became the first fairways. Early golf courses were built along the high bluffs of Scotland's eastern coastline, where strong winds and the tide had formed natural dunes, ridges, and gullies that challenged players. A game of golf was often followed by a visit to the local tavern, and bets were placed on the sport, which had become quite popular in Scotland by the 15th century.

The first documented reference to golf dates from 1457, when King James II of Scotland signed an edict banning the sport, because he felt that playing golf distracted men from their archery, which all adult men were supposed to practice daily, in preparation for war. The game was, however, enjoyed by both the Scottish and English royal houses, which is why the sport is often called "the royal and ancient game." Mary, Queen of Scots, enjoyed the sport, and her critics complained that she was out "playing golf in the fields by Seton" when she should have been mourning the death of her husband in 1567. One of the first known caddies, a young boy, worked for the Duke of York (later James II), carrying his clubs and running ahead to announce where the balls fell.

*In this 17th-century painting by J.C. Dollman, entitled* During the Times of the Sermones, *a village pastor and deacon discover two Scottish men playing golf instead of attending church.*

In the 17th and 18th centuries, golf was played primarily by affluent club members in Scotland. In 1744, the Magistrates and Council of Edinburgh approved the first rules and regulations of match play golf, which were drawn up by the gentlemen golfers of Leith:

1. You must tee your ball within a club-length of the hole.

2. Your tee must be upon the ground.

3. You are not to change the ball which you strike off the tee.

4. You are not to remove stones, bones, or anything for the sake of playing your ball, except on the fair green, and then only that within a club's length of your ball.

5. If your ball comes among water, or any watery filth, you are at liberty to take out your ball and throw it behind the hazard; you may play it with any club, and allow your adversary a stroke for so getting out your ball.

6. If your balls be found anywhere touching each other, you are to lift the first ball until you play the last.

7. At holing you are to play your ball honestly for the hole, and not to play upon your adversary's ball.

8. If you should lose your ball by its being taken up, or any other way, you are to go back to the spot where you struck last and drop another ball and allow your adversary a stroke for this misfortune.

9. No man at holing his ball is to be allowed to mark his way to the hole with his club or anything else.

10. If a ball is stopped by any person, horse, or dog, or anything else, the ball so stopped must be played where it lies.

11. If you draw your club in order to strike and proceed so far in your stroke as to bring down your club, and your club breaks in any way, it is counted as a stroke.

12. He whose ball lies farthest from the hole is obliged to play first.

13. Neither trench, ditch, or dyke made for the preservation of the links shall be counted as a hazard, but the ball is to be taken out, teed, and played with any iron club.

The Society of St. Andrews golfers, whose records date from 1754, agreed to play by these same 13 rules. Under the aegis of King William IV in 1854, the society took the name "The Royal and Ancient Golf Club of St. Andrews." This club dominated the subsequent development and standardization of golf and became recognized as the governing body of world golf. Its first tournament on record was held in Prestwick on the western coast of Scotland in 1860. Later, when the competition was opened to anyone who wanted to play, it became known as the British Open. In its earliest form, the Open Championship consisted of man-to-man match play, with three rounds of 12 holes. When stroke-play golf came into being, St. Andrews arbitrarily adopted a round of eighteen holes, setting the standard for all other courses.

The rules of golf have changed very little since the end of the 19th century, but golf equipment has changed tremendously. Before the invention of the golf tee in Scotland in 1889, golfers drove balls off mounds of sand. Some of the earliest golf balls were "featheries," consisting of boiled feathers tightly stuffed into small leather bags that had a

*Wooden balls were used in the early history of golf, but they were replaced by "featheries," tiny sacks of leather stuffed with boiled feathers. Later, balls known as "gutties" were made from gutta percha, the sap from rubber trees.*

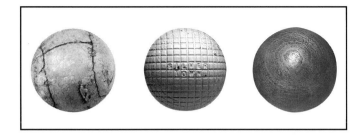

driving range of up to 175 yards. After 1848, balls made of gutta percha, a hard rubber-like substance made from the sap of Malayasian trees, came into use. These "gutty" balls were far superior to featheries, and could be driven as far as 225 yards. In 1898, the rubber-cored golf ball, invented in the United States, came into popular use. It consisted of a gutta percha shell enclosing a ball of rubber thread wound under tension around a solid rubber core. This new ball flew farther and increased the enjoyment of the game. In 1932, the United States Golf Association (USGA) approved the standard 1.62 ounce ball and sanctioned a minimum diameter of 1.68 inches.

Golf bags did not come into use until around 1860; prior to that, a caddie carried all the player's clubs by balancing them on one shoulder. Early clubs were carved from wood. Players might use one club for several types of strokes. Before the development of the pitching wedge, players caught in sand traps lofted the ball with a "baffing spoon," using the flat sole of the club to strike the ground near the ball. Then, as the ball rebounded off the turf, they hit it in mid-air. Gradually, clubs with iron heads and varying degrees of loft were developed for the different situations where a golf ball might lie.

In 1910 the steel shaft was patented in the U.S., replacing the old hand-shaped wooden shafts. Steel shafts could be mass produced, making clubs less expensive. Golf balls were designed to go farther, and golf clubs engineered to reduce the effects of the slice and hook. In 1938 the USGA imposed a limit of 14 clubs per player, and the following year Scotland's Royal and Ancient Golf Club followed suit. The limit was imposed to keep golf a test of skill, and a game whose outcome was dependent on swing and control rather than which player had the greatest variety of clubs.

Although Americans have been responsible for many of the substantial improvements in technology and equipment over the years, the history of golf owes much to the Scottish pioneers. It was these first players whom Dr. Benjamin Rush referred to in 1770, when he said of the game: "Golf is an exercise which is much used by the gentlemen in Scotland. A large common, in which there are several little holes, is chosen for this purpose. It is played with little leather balls stuffed with feathers, and sticks tipped with horn. He who putts with the fewest strokes gets the game . . . A man would live ten years the longer for using this exercise once or twice a week." The Scottish players' devotion and enthusiasm for the game helped foster its growth.

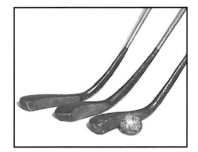

*These wooden long-nosed golf clubs, which look like modern-day hockey sticks, date from the 1800s.*

# PIONEERS OF THE GAME

**3**

One of the pioneers of golf in early 19th century Scotland was Allan Robertson, a ball-maker, keeper of the links at St. Andrews, and a renowned golfer who could control his shots with near-scientific accuracy. Robertson had grown up at St. Andrews and learned the ball-making trade and the game from his father. Allan Robertson is credited with introducing iron clubs for approach play, and with helping to develop some of the finest names in golf.

A young protégé of Robertson's, "Old Tom" Morris, became a leading figure of golf in the 19th century. As a youngster, "Old Tom" apprenticed in Robertson's featherie-making shop and eventually teamed up with Robertson to compete in stakes matches throughout Scotland. Morris's success caused him to be matched with another skilled Scottish golfer, Willie Park, and the two men began a nearly life-long series of hotly contested matches.

In 1870, one of their competitions, a four-course, multi-round match that drew hundreds of spectators, began at St. Andrews, then moved to Prestwick and on to North Berwick before finally culminating at Musselburgh, Scotland. The match was close, with no more than one or two holes separating the two golfers. But during the final round, which took place on a cold day in heavy rain, the crowd grew unruly. As the rain poured, the horde of spectators closed in on the

*The Royal and Ancient Golf Club of St. Andrews, Scotland dominated the early development of golf and became recognized as the world's governing body of golf.*

golfers, and Park and Morris barely had room to swing their clubs. With Park at a two-hole lead, the two men decided to break for a drink at a nearby lodge, hoping the crowd would settle down. Willie Park came out soon afterward to finish the course, but Old Tom Morris did not. He remained indoors, claiming he had asked the referee for a postponement, based on the behavior of the crowd. Upon hearing this, Park was extremely agitated and claimed Morris had never consulted him. He finished playing and proclaimed himself the winner. Morris finished his game the next day, by himself, and the referee declared him the winner. Park and Morris never settled the controversy between them, and it went on for years.

Morris, who maintained the greens at Prestwick, helped to organize the first Open Championship in 1860. Willie Park took the title the first year, but Old Tom Morris won three of the next four Opens. At age 46, Old Tom became the oldest golfer to win the British Open. His son, "Young Tom" Morris, was a golf prodigy who won his first Open at age 17 and went on to win it three more times in a row before his untimely death at age 24. He remains the only player to have won four consecutive British Opens.

Despite the popularity of golf in Scotland, the sport did not immediately arouse widespread interest in Britain. As Horace Hutchinson, the British golf writer, noted: "If you announced yourself a golfer, people stared at you. What did it mean? Oh yes! That Scotch game—like hockey, was it not like polo? Did you play it on horseback? . . . In general people had never seen the weapons before, and asked you, with an

*Harry Vardon, shown here lining up a putt, never played with more than six clubs. The Vardon trophies, awarded on both the PGA and European Tours for low scoring average, were named in his memory.*

apology for their inquisitiveness, what their use could be . . . Or if people did know a little of the game, then their regards were no longer curious but pitiful, as who would say, "See the poor loony—is he not a sad sight?" It grew common to regard golf as a harmless form of imbecility, holding towards it much the same attitude that the general mind has towards a grown man with a butterfly net and a taste for entomology."

The history of golf owes much to the earliest players who succeeded in popularizing the

*James Braid was a clubmaker in Scotland when he turned professional and took the golf world by storm, winning the British Open five times. Later, Braid turned to designing and remodeling golf courses.*

game in Europe. Among the first names in golf were "The Great Triumvirate"—Harry Vardon, James Braid, and John Henry Taylor, who between them won the British Open 16 times in 20 years. Harry Vardon, an Englishman, had an upright, unexaggerated swing and could hit the ball straighter than any of his rivals. His swing was analyzed and copied by his many admirers. Vardon, known as a master of iron shots, also popularized the overlapping grip, in which the pinky and index fingers are entwined while grasping the club. This grip, which provides a maximum of leverage at the moment the ball is struck, remains the grip used by the majority of golfers today. Vardon won six British Opens and the 1900 U.S. Open.

James Braid, a Scotsman, was a clubmaker-turned-professional golfer who won the British Open five times. His unusual swing included a dip of his knees through impact, yet he was such a long hitter he often used a one-iron to maintain control. In his later years, Braid became an accomplished golf course builder, designing over 122 courses and remodeling another 57.

John Henry, or "J. H." Taylor, was another Briton who began golfing as a youngster. A caddie-turned-professional, Taylor won five British Opens with his unusual swing, which golf writer Bernard Darwin described: "It was not what we had been brought up to think of as a swing. It was a flick or a punch, delivered markedly firm-footed, with little obvious follow-through. It was impressive, fascinating and in its straightness positively demonical." After his playing career, J. H. Taylor helped found and oversee the British PGA and lobbied for the creation of more public golf courses in Britain.

The early successes of these Scottish and English players helped stir an interest in golf among Americans. Scottish immigrants, who are credited with being the first to transplant golf to America, brought with them an enthusiasm for golf that soon infected the continent.

# 4

# GOLF COMES TO AMERICA

One of the first people to bring golf clubs and balls stateside was Robert Lockhart, a New York linen merchant originally from Scotland. Lockhart's business required him to make frequent trips to his home country, and on one of these visits he bought a set of clubs and two dozen gutta percha balls from the shop of Old Tom Morris. Lockhart gave the golf clubs and balls to his friend, John Reid, another transplanted Scotsman. Sharing the set of clubs between them, Reid and his friends played every Sunday.

In 1888, Reid, who is known as the father of American golf, founded the first American golf club—St. Andrew's Golf Club in Yonkers, New York. The six-hole course had dusty greens, and the cups were scooped out with clubs. Three-foot-high wooden stakes, topped with numbered metal plates, functioned as flagpoles. Since there were no golf bags at this time, caddies carried all the clubs in a bundle on their shoulder.

The popularity of the sport grew, prompting the *New York Times* to write in 1895: "In the history of American field sports there can be found no outdoor pastime that developed and attained such popularity in such a relatively short period of time." By the turn of the century, there were more than 1000 golf courses in the nation, with Massachusetts and New York each hosting over 150. Other early clubs included the Tuxedo Golf

*As the gallery watches, Walter Hagen, known for his fashionable attire, retrieves his ball on the 18th hole at the 1919 U.S. Open.*

Club in New York (1889), the Newport Golf Club in Rhode Island (1890), the Middlesboro Golf Club in Kentucky (1890), and the Hotel Champlain Golf Course in New York (1890).

In 1894 a group of eastern golfers organized the first U.S. Open, hosted by St. Andrew's. Later that year, members from some of the country's first golf clubs got together to form the United States Golf Association (USGA). The USGA's purpose was to establish uniformity in the rules of play, provide a court of reference in matters of controversy, and determine where championships would be held. More than 100 years later, the USGA continues to be the controlling body for golf in America.

In 1895, one year after the formation of the USGA, a group of women golfers organized the first USGA Women's Amateur championship, held to recognize a growing female interest in the sport.

Since coming to America from Scotland in the late 19th century, golf has been dominated by whites, but the history of blacks in golf dates from same time. In 1899, Dr. George Grant, a black dentist and Harvard graduate, patented the first golf tee in the U.S.

Another black man, John Shippen, who taught golf at Shinnecock golf course on Long Island, N.Y., made waves in 1896 by competing in his first U.S. Open. The other entrants, who were white and predominantly foreign, threatened to boycott the tournament if Shippen and another golfer, Oscar Bunn, a Native American, were allowed to play. USGA president Theodore Havermyer, however, insisted that the Open would be held, even if Shippen and Bunn were the only players, and the objectors reluctantly agreed to play.

Following World War I, more African-Americans began playing golf, although public golf courses placed many restrictions on where and when they could play. In 1926 a group of black doctors from Washington D.C. formed the United Golfers Association and held their first tournament at Mapledale, an all-black country club in Boston. The UGA promoted the sport by inviting black golfers like Jim Brown, Joe Louis, and Jackie Robinson to play on its circuit.

The first U.S. amateur to come to the foreground was Walter Travis, who in 1904 became the first American to win the British Amateur Championship. Then, in 1913, at the U.S. Open, a young man named Francis Ouimet did what Tiger Woods did by winning the Masters in 1997: he took golf to the front page of America's newspapers by defeating two established English golf stars, Harry Vardon and Ted Ray.

Ouimet's victory ushered in a whole new era for the game. Suddenly, everyone wanted to play golf. More public courses were laid out in American cities, and more and more people joined golf clubs. An increasing number of amateur golfers turned professional, leading to the formation of the Professional Golfers' Association (PGA) and its annual championship in 1916. By the 1920s the golf craze had made the golf "look" fashionable—baggy knickers, two-toned golf shoes, Argyle vests, and blazers were in.

Golf enthusiasts in the U.S. and Great Britain also organized the first international golf contests between the two countries: the Ryder Cup, Walker Cup, and Curtis Cup matches. The Walker Cup, presented by George H. Walker, former president of the USGA, is awarded to the winner of an international amateur competition, held every two years. The Ryder Cup, presented by Samuel Ryder, a supporter of British professional golf, goes to the winner of the professional competition, which is also held biennially. The Curtis Cup was donated in 1927 by two women from Boston, sisters Harriot and Margaret Curtis, who had previously traveled to England to play in the British Ladies Championships. In 1932, biennial Curtis Cup Matches began between amateur women's teams.

One of the most prominent American golfers from 1923 to 1930 was Robert Tyre Jones Jr., or Bobby Jones, an amateur golfer who won the 1923 U.S. Open at the age of 21. Between 1924 and 1929, Jones won three U.S. Amateurs, two British Opens, and two U.S. Opens. As an amateur, Jones defeated many pro players, much to their embarrassment. His prowess caused established pro golfer Walter Hagen to tell his colleagues, "We've got to stop this kid."

In 1930 Jones achieved unparalleled success and entered the annals of golf history by winning what was then golf's Grand Slam: both the British and U.S. Opens as well as the U.S. and British Amateurs. Jones, who remained an amateur throughout his career, is the only golfer to have ever won a Grand Slam. Known as the boy-wonder from Atlanta, Georgia, Jones and his famous wooden putter, which he called "Calamity Jane," retired at the age of 28, after dominating nearly ever championship for a decade. Following his sensational year in 1930, Warner Brothers signed Jones to produce an instructional series of short films called "How I Play Golf," which included some of the biggest motion picture stars of the 1930s. These were among the first Hollywood films about golf.

*Bobby Jones, the "Boy Wonder" from Atlanta, played golf only a few months out of the year and spent most of his time studying engineering, literature, and law. Yet in 1930, Jones became the only golfer to have ever won the Grand Slam. Despite his unparalleled success, Jones remained an amateur throughout his career and retired at age 28.*

After he retired, Jones went on to enjoy a successful career as a golf course architect and is best known for his work in co-founding Georgia's Augusta National golf course, where the inaugural Masters tournament was held in 1934. To design his "dream" course, Jones teamed up with famed Scottish golf course architect, Dr. Alistar MacKenzie, and after a long search for the ideal location, the two men settled on Augusta, the hometown of Jones's wife, Mary. Today, Augusta National remains an enduring legacy from one of golf's great champions.

In 1997 the international voting body for the World Golf Hall of Fame, which consists of journalists and golf officials, selected Jones's 1930 Grand Slam as the greatest moment in golf history. According to PGA pro Tom Watson, "Bobby Jones represents the kind of golfer and the kind of person that all Tour professionals aspire to be. What he accomplished in 1930 and throughout his career may never be matched."

The flamboyant Walter Hagen, with his slicked-back hair, plus fours (baggy knickers) and black and white shoes, brought a sense of style and playfulness to golf in the teens and twenties. A master of "psyching out" his opponents, Hagen would stand on the first tee and declare loudly, "I wonder who's going to take second."

Regarded as the man who taught the world how to putt, Hagen was especially renowned for his ability to make shots under pressure. In 1922 he became the first American-born player to win the British Open, ushering in a series of American wins for this title. Walter Hagen was

*Byron Nelson, shown lining up a putt, set the record for the winningest streak in golf history in 1945 when he won 18 tournaments, 11 of them consecutive. Nelson's streak, which has never been surpassed, also came with an all time low scoring average of 68.33.*

also the first golfer to win four consecutive PGA tournaments.

When Hagen won his fifth PGA in Dallas in 1927, a young boy named Byron Nelson was watching from the gallery. On that day, Nelson decided that he'd rather be a professional golfer than a baseball player. 11 years later, he completed the winningest streak in golf history. From March 11 to August 4, 1945, Byron Nelson won each of the 11 tournaments that he entered.

The standards for prize money grew along with the popularity of the sport. Nelson's winning streak earned him $30,000 in 1945; the same streak 50 years later would earn around two million dollars. Pioneers like Harry Vardon, James Braid, and J.H. Taylor earned only about 30 pounds ($48) for taking first place. Byron Nelson and Ben Hogan signed for $1500 each in the 1930s. In 1954, Arnold Palmer, golf's first television star, earned $2000 a month from Wilson Sporting Goods,

*Shown here in his trademark hat, Samuel Jackson Snead emerged from the Virginia countryside in the 1930s, beginning a tour career that would span four decades. "Slammin' Sammy," as he was called, had one of the most prolific careers in golf, winning 84 times between 1936 and 1965 and setting the record (81) for the most official PGA Tour wins.*

and Jack Nicklaus got $100,000 from MacGregor equipment in 1961.

Just before war broke out in Europe, another great American golfer, Samuel Jackson Snead, emerged from the Virginia countryside in 1937 and began a tour career that lasted more than 40 years. Snead, who earned the nickname "Slammin' Sammy" as a kid, began playing in the woods around his home with a club fashioned from a tree limb. He quickly learned to shape shots and to hit the ball straight and long.

Snead had one of the greatest careers of any pro golfer. He won a record 81 official PGA tour victories, including the 1949, 1952, and 1954 Masters, as well as three PGA Championships (1942, 1949, 1951) and the 1946 British Open. In 1949, Snead was the first Masters Champion to be awarded a green jacket, inaugurating a tradition that continues to the present

*As golf increased in popularity in America, it was also becoming popular around the world, where differences in environment provided interesting challenges on the course. This golf course in Elizabethville, Congo, boasts 120 giant anthills around which players must maneuver.*

day. In addition to his PGA victories, Snead won 185 other pro tournaments.

"[Snead] always had the gift of good vision and a keen kinesthetic awareness of what he had to do to hit a particular shot," says neuropsychologist Dr. Fran Pirozzolo, who works with golfers on the mental aspect of their game and recently wrote a book with Snead. "He could hit, for example, a big high hook, and then cut a little shot into a green. He did a lot of visualization."

Despite his amazing abilities, Snead, like many golfers, never won a U.S. Open. After birdieing the last hole at the 1937 U.S. Open to finish with a 71, Snead watched his chance at victory disappear when Ralph Guldahl came in with a two-shot lead. While Snead looked on, Guldahl paused to comb his hair at the final green, in preparation for the photographers, then finished his game with a 69. After the game, Snead said, "All at once it got real lonesome where I was standing. You could have shot off an elephant gun in my corner of the locker room and not winged a single sportswriter."

Snead is also remembered as the only golfer to have lost a tournament because he hit a shot into the men's bathroom. At the Cleveland Open, Snead sailed one through the open door of the men's locker room, where it ricocheted into the men's bathroom. Snead incurred a two-point penalty for this shot and lost the tournament by one stroke.

Golf stars like Samuel Snead, Bobby Jones, Byron Nelson, Walter Hagen, and Francis Ouimet gave the game a boost during its first half-century in America. The formation of golf organizations like the United States Golf

Association (USGA) and the Professional Golfers Association (PGA), and the creation of popular tournaments also helped sponsor the rapid growth of the game in America. By the 1940s there were over 6,000 golf courses in America and millions of new players.

# THE GROWTH OF AMERICAN GOLF

**5**

The postwar years saw the rise of many new golf stars and an increased American interest in the game. The new medium of television brought golf into American living rooms. Golf enthusiasts could now watch their favorite players and study their swings. President Dwight Eisenhower, an avid golfer, helped to popularize the sport. And for the first time, women and African-Americans began to make serious progress as professional golfers. In 1971 the first man to walk on the moon, American Alan Shepard, brought along a six-iron and made a shot for America.

One of the most successful professional golfers to emerge in the postwar era was Ben Hogan, the "mighty mite" of golf. A meticulous golfer, Hogan would pick the course apart, divide it into inches, and decide on the best routes to play each hole. "Management," he believed, "is 80 percent of winning." This philosophy worked for Hogan, who won four U.S. Opens, two Masters, one British Open, and his second PGA Championship, all between 1948 and 1957.

Hogan's story is all the more sensational for the adversity he encountered. After a nearly fatal car crash in 1949, in which his pelvis, collarbone, ribs and ankle were broken, doctors were uncertain whether Hogan would ever play golf again. Determined to overcome his injuries, Hogan entered the U.S. Open that year but was too weak to play. In 1950, however, his legs

*Ben Hogan, shown following through with his drive, came closer to winning the modern Grand Slam than any other golfer. In 1953 he won the first three legs, the Masters, U.S. Open, and British Open. However, Hogan failed to return from Great Britain in time to play in the final leg, the PGA Championship.*

bandaged from ankle to groin, Hogan played in and won the U.S. Open. In 1953 he won the triple crown of golf: the Masters, the U.S. Open and the British Open. Hogan's remarkable comeback inspired *Follow the Sun*, a movie about his life.

Women, who had joined the war effort and entered the labor force in record numbers during World War II, began to gain more credibility and equality with men in the years following the war. Similarly, women's golf began to make greater strides as the Ladies Professional Golf Association (LPGA) promoted its circuit. One of the first women to garner widespread attention for women's golf was the multi-talented Mildred "Babe" Didrikson Zaharias. A veritable one-woman track team

*Mildred "Babe" Didrikson Zaharias excelled at every sport she tried. After winning several medals in track and field at the 1932 Olympics, Babe took up golf and led the money list from 1948 to 1951. "I just loosen my girdle and let the ball have it," she explained when asked about her ability to make drives over 250 yards. In 1949 Babe helped found the Ladies Professional Golf Association (LPGA) with fellow golfer Patty Berg.*

*Patty Berg has won more majors than any other woman, with a total of 15 Grand Slam titles. Berg helped found the Ladies Professional Golf Association (LPGA) in 1949 and became the organization's first president.*

and star of the 1932 Olympics, Zaharias excelled at every sport she tried. Putting her hand to golf, she won 40 tournaments in less than four years, including the 1946 U.S. Amateur and the 1947 British Amateur. Concerned about opportunities for women in golf, she joined forces with Patty Berg to help found the Ladies Professional Golf Association in 1949.

Patty Berg, who became the LPGA's first president, set the record for winning the most majors in women's golf, with one U.S. Open, seven Titleholders championships, and seven Western Opens under her belt. (The Western Open and Titleholders Championships, once the major tournaments in women's golf, were discontinued, however, in the 1960s and '70s, and the women's Grand Slam events became the U.S. Open, LPGA Championship, Du Maurier Classic, and the Nabisco Dinah Shore.) Other key figures in the growing credibility of professional women's golf were Mickey Wright, whose 82 career victories include 13 major

*In 1957 Charles Sifford became the first African-American to win the Long Beach Open, a predominantly white event. Sifford was also the first black man to win a major PGA event, the Hartford Open in 1967.*

titles and numerous records, and Kathy Whitworth, who won more tournaments (88) than any player, man or woman.

But unlike men's golf, women's golf in the 1950s and '60s remained a hand-to-mouth business. Women traveled the fledgling tour circuit by car, often sharing expenses and living out of their automobiles. To supplement their prize money, female golfers hosted clinics and exhibitions. The early LPGA stars were a dedicated bunch. Betsy Rawls, who played the LPGA tour from 1951 to 1975, continued to contribute to the game following her retirement by serving as LPGA tour director for six years. Another early LPGA star, Louise Suggs, served as LPGA president for three terms, joining ranks with Zaharias, Berg, Rawls, and the other dedicated women who helped promote the LPGA.

The postwar period also marked the rise of African-Americans in golf. Initially excluded from most golf courses except as caddies (a "Caucasian only" law existed in the PGA by-laws until 1961), blacks began to make inroads as professional golfers. Charles Sifford, who won five consecutive National Negro Championships from 1952 to 1956, was among the first to challenge elitism and racism in golf. "I found out I could smack a golf ball and make it go straight and far. And once I learned that, nothing was going to stop me from playing the game and getting better," Sifford later wrote in his autobiography, *Just Let Me Play.*

Sifford endured discrimination, harassment, and physical threats to play on fairways that didn't want him. "You could back a million

*Known and beloved by fans for his grimaces and smiles, part of Arnold Palmer's appeal is the way he lets his emotions show during the game. Here Palmer stares the ball in for a birdie at the 1971 Citrus Invitational.*

people against the wall, white or black," said Sifford, who, in his 70s, still competed. "Nobody would have gone through what I did—just to be a golfer." Though he twice won professional tour events in the 1960s, Sifford was told each time that he was not good enough to compete in the Masters. "When I was playing, they had people running the Masters who thought it was beneficial for blacks not to play there," said Sifford. An unusual and changing scoring system that specified which golfers qualified for the Masters was used to keep blacks out of the competition. "They kept changing the rules on me," Sifford said, "They changed the rules [for qualifying] when I won my first tournament and they changed the rules again when I won my second."

Sifford's footsteps were followed by Lee Elder, who broke the color barrier when he became the first black man invited to the Masters in Augusta, Georgia, in 1975. In addition, Elder's score of 61—11 under par—at the 1985 Merrill Lynch/Golf Digest Commemorative was the lowest score ever recorded on the senior tour.

With his audacity, his trademark pants-hitch, his final-round charges, and his hordes of adoring fans, Arnold Palmer became the first television icon of golf. Palmer was a graduate of Wake Forest, one of many colleges and universities to establish golf teams in the 1950s. The first golfer to reach $1 million in career earnings, Palmer won four Masters, two British Opens and one U.S. Open between the years 1958 and 1964. In the prime of his career, he drew crowds of up to 30,000 spectators. Part of Palmer's appeal was the way he allowed his emotions to show. Spectators could see, and empathize with, his elation or despair. Known for making impossible shots and coming from behind to win, Palmer confirmed his reputation at the 1960 U.S. Open. Seven shots behind the leader with a final round to play, Palmer had a brief conversation with his friend Bob Drum, a journalist covering the event. "What would happen if I shot a 65?" Palmer asked him.

"Nothing," Drum replied, "You're out of it."

"The hell I am," Palmer roared. "A 65 would give me 280, and 280 is the kind of score that usually wins the Open."

Energized, Palmer went back to the course for the final round, drove to the green on the par-four first hole, birdied six of the next seven holes, and finished with 65 to win the tournament.

Palmer was also the first golfer on the Senior PGA tour to make holes-in-one on consecutive days. During the Chrysler Cup Senior PGA Tour, Palmer aced the 187-yard third hole at TPC Avenue Course near Washington D.C. The next day he did it again, although the odds of this happening were calculated at 9 million to one.

Palmer's greatest rival, Jack Nicklaus, emerged on the pro golf scene in 1962, at age 22. Like Palmer, Nicklaus had played golf in college, and he was an impressive opponent for the famous Palmer. Arnie's army of fans were harsh on the young Nicklaus, who was dubbed the "Golden Bear" for his blond hair

*Jack Nicklaus, dubbed the "Golden Bear," has won 18 Grand Slam titles—more than any other golfer—with 6 Masters, 4 U.S. Opens, 3 British Opens, and 5 PGA Championships to his name.*

and youthful chubbiness, but Nicklaus's sheer skill soon brought him his own loyal following. Setting his sights on the big championships, Nicklaus was determined to break Bobby Jones's record of 13 majors. Considered by many to be the greatest golfer that ever lived, Nicklaus succeeded in his quest, winning 20 major titles: six Masters (a record), five PGA Championships, four U.S. Opens, three British Opens, and two U.S. Amateur Championships. His first Masters victory came in 1963 when he was just 23 years old, and for 17 years he held the record for being the youngest to win the Masters. And in 1986 Nicklaus came from behind to shoot a 65 on the final round at Augusta, making him, at age 46, the oldest man to win the Masters. In addition, Nicklaus's 271 four-day record total at Augusta, matched only by Ray Floyd in 1976, stood as a Masters record until Tiger Woods came along in 1997 with a 270.

Both Nicklaus and Palmer found a stiff competitor in Gary Player, a South African golfer known for dressing in black, who became the first foreign golfer to achieve great success in the United States. Between 1958 and 1979, Player won three Masters, two PGA Championships, a U.S. Open, and three British Opens. He was also the first foreigner to win a Masters.

Known as the "Big Three," Nicklaus, Palmer, and Gary Player dominated golf in the 1960s and '70s, but the 1980s and '90s brought new, record-breaking talent to the golf scene.

# 6    THE MODERN STARS

**W**ith Americans spending over $1.37 billion on golf clubs alone in 1996, golf had grown into a major industry by the end of the 20th century. Golf stars became marketable for multi-million dollar endorsement deals. Tournament prize money continued to escalate. The image of golf also changed from an elite sport played by the well-heeled to a game popular among people of all ages, classes, and skills. But those who made it to the top of the PGA and LPGA tours—the professional men and women who devoted their lives to the sport— remained a cut above, separated by their talent and dedication.

In 1997 he was the man who lost to Tiger Woods at the Masters, but Tom Kite earned $291,600 for his second place finish. Known as "Mr. Consistency" for his steady wins, the 46-year-old Kite was the second player in PGA tour history to exceed $10 million in career earnings. With a total of $10,018,007 in 1997, Kite ranked just below all-time leading money winner Greg Norman, who headed the list with $10,553,219 in career earnings. After playing on seven Ryder Cup teams and winning 60 percent of his cup matches, Tom Kite was named captain of the American team for the 1997 match in Spain. Kite immediately picked Tiger Woods for the team.

*Tom Kite, runner-up to Tiger Woods at the Masters, was chosen to captain the 1997 Ryder Cup team. Called "Mr. Consistency" for his steady wins, Kite was the second PGA pro to earn more than $10 million.*

During much of 1997, Australian-born Greg Norman was the top-ranked golf player in the world. Norman learned the rudiments of the game while caddying for his mother, who was an avid golfer, in Australia. At age 21 he turned professional. Norman won 29 world tournaments before joining the American tour. Also a winner of two British Opens, Norman was named the PGA Player of the Year in 1995, and he earned three Arnold Palmer awards and three Vardon trophies for his low scoring average.

Known as the "Great White Shark" because of his love for deep-sea fishing and his blond hair, Greg Norman turned his nickname into an industry, Great White Shark Enterprises, which designs golf courses and provides course turf. An accomplished businessman, Norman successfully converted his public appeal into revenue, setting an example for other sports stars to follow. Despite his financial success, Norman is remembered more for at least one playoff loss in each of the major tournaments. At the 1996 Masters, Norman led the field by six strokes but collapsed in a dramatic final round, losing to England's Nick Faldo.

Another top-ranked golfer, Nick Faldo was 14 when he first saw Jack Nicklaus playing in a televised Masters tournament. The next day he asked his mother for golf lessons. Faldo, who turned professional at age 19, was the youngest person ever named to Britain's Ryder Cup team. In 1990 Faldo also became the first international player to win the PGA tour's Player of the Year award. From 1993 to 1994, Faldo led the Sony world golf rankings for 81 consecutive weeks. Through 1996, Faldo had won six major titles—three Masters and three British Opens. At the 1996 Masters, Faldo shot a final round of 67 to win by five strokes.

Known as the "Iceman" for his austere demeanor and ability to concentrate, Faldo was at one time one of the most unpopular players on the PGA tour. However, Faldo, who won the PGA Player of the Year award in 1990, worked to improve his image. "Before, I never thought about anything except golf," he admitted. "Now I have a family, and they mean the most to me . . . you get wiser as you get older. I've learned to lighten up."

Faldo made golf history in 1990 when he hired Fanny Sunesson, the first full-time female caddie on the men's professional tour. A caddie carries a player's golf bag and is the only person a golfer can consult for advice on which club to use or which shot to play. A caddie's actions also reflect on the player, for if he or she interferes with an opponent's ball, the player incurs the penalties. Caddies on the men's tour have traditionally been male, and many male golfers doubted a woman's ability to give sound advice and carry a full golf bag over 18 holes. But, like many aspects of golf, this too is changing.

One of the strongest all-around golfers with the best scoring average on the PGA tour in 1996 was Tom Lehman, who won the British Open and TOUR Championship, receiving 1996 Player of the Year honors. A 1995 Ryder Cup team player, Lehman was third in the '93 Masters and second in 1994. Lehman also placed well at the 1997 U.S. Open, which was won by Ernie Els. Hailing from South Africa,

Els is one of the PGA's most talented young players. At twenty-seven, his tour victories already include two U.S. Opens (1994 and 1997) and three successive World Matchplay titles. In 1994 Els was named Rookie of the Year after ranking in the top 20 on four of the world's tours: the PGA tour, the European tour, the Austral/Asian tour, and the South African tour.

LPGA hall-of-famer Nancy Lopez, a four-time winner of the LPGA Player of the Year award, began golfing as a little girl in New Mexico and dropped out of college in 1977 to turn professional. Though she had an unorthodox swing that looped on its way to the top, it worked for her. In her rookie year in 1978 when she was just 21, Lopez became the Tiger Woods of her generation. With her father, Domingo, there to back her up, Lopez won five tournaments in a row—a total of nine that year—and took home an LPGA record $189,813, which was more than any rookie—male or female—had ever earned. She also won Player of the Year and Rookie of the Year honors, as well as the Vare trophy for low scoring average. Lopez made women's golf exciting. The following year she won eight times and received Player of the Year and Vare honors again. Lopez became only the fifth LPGA pro to exceed $1 million in career earnings.

Karrie Webb, a 21-year-old Australian, drew comparisons to a young Nancy Lopez when she won the women's British Open in 1995 and four LPGA events in 1996. Webb became the first woman to win over $1 million dollars in a single season. The young Webb, whose job sweeping floors in her mother's café did not earn her enough funds to turn pro, borrowed $5,000 from her grandparents to take the plunge. Her first year paid off. Nancy Lopez has praised young Webb's attitude on the course "[She's] not intimidated by anything or anybody."

Known for her striking broad-brimmed sun hats, Michelle McGann is another young standout on the LPGA tour. McGann joined the tour at age 19, right out of high school, and was the youngest player on the tour by four years. Eight years later, a 27-year-old McGann, nicknamed "The Queen," led the tour

*Greg Norman, the "Great White Shark" of golf, caddied for his mother before turning professional at age 21. In 1997, Norman was the top-ranked player in the world.*

in birdies and was second in driving distance with her powerful 255-yard average. In 1995 McGann won the Sara Lee Classic, setting off a string of victories for herself. "As soon as I won that first one," McGann admits, "it was like a big weight lifted off my shoulders. Now I feel like I can win every time I tee it up." Ninth on the LPGA money list, McGann was ranked just behind Nancy Lopez in 1997.

Another young champion, Sweden's 26-year-old Annika Sorenstam, has come to the forefront of women's golf. Winner of two consecutive U.S. Opens, Sorenstam joined the LPGA in 1993. By 1995 she topped the LPGA and the Women's Professional Golf European Tour (WPGET) money rankings. Sorenstam was one of only three women to receive LPGA Rookie of the Year and Player of the Year honors in consecutive years (1994 and 1995).

"The standard [for the LPGA] just gets better and better," says LPGA pro Laura Davies. "And I think it's going to keep getting better from this point onward. All the young players see us playing on TV, and they want to come out and beat us."

Despite its recent boom, women's golf has never enjoyed the widespread recognition that men's golf has achieved, and this is upsetting to LPGA professionals like Nancy Lopez. "I get really bummed out when I see women's beach volleyball on television. Do we have to wear bikinis to get people to watch us? The LPGA has some great players and some great minds." But things are looking up for women golfers. In 1996, under the direction of LPGA Commissioner Jim Ritts, four new tournaments were added for the 1997 roster and prize money was increased by twenty percent. The LPGA has also continued to cultivate new, younger players.

To help involve more young women in golf, the LPGA created partnerships with the USGA and the Girl Scouts of the U.S.A. to expand its Girls Golf Club program. Designed to introduce girls aged 7–17 to golf, the program invites LPGA tour players to serve as tour captains for the clubs. Over 40 LPGA tour players participate in the Girls Golf Club program.

Golf champions continue to get younger and younger. At 21, Tiger Woods had assured

*Known as the "Iceman" for his stern manner on the course, England's Nick Faldo concentrates on his game while checking out the line for a shot.*

himself a place in the annals of golf history, but Woods was already a golf prodigy when he was 3 years old and broke 50 for nine holes, golfing with his father. From age 15, he won three consecutive U.S. Junior Amateur titles (1991, 1992, and 1993) and then three straight U.S. Amateurs (1994, 1995, and 1996).

An agent from International Management Group (IMG) began to follow Woods when he was just 13. As an amateur, he signed endorsement deals worth more than $50 million dollars with Nike and Titleist and became one of the hottest athletes in the world. In 1996 he dropped out of Stanford University to join the PGA tour, winning two of the eight tourneys he played that year. *Sports Illustrated* writer Gary Van Sickle predicted, "Golf, as we know it, is over. It came to an end on a chamber-of-commerce Sunday evening in Las Vegas when Tiger Woods went for the upgrade: He's not just a promising young Tour pro anymore, he's an era." If anyone had doubts about Tiger Woods, they were put to rest when he won the Masters in 1997.

"All I want is the green jacket," Woods claimed during his assault on Augusta National, but he made a few records for himself along the way. At age 21, Woods earned his fourth major—something no other golfer had done. Jack Nicklaus had only 2 majors by age 21, and Bobby Jones had only one at that age. Tiger's 12-stroke victory margin was also the greatest in modern golf. Not since the days of Old and Young Tom Morris had anyone won by such a generous margin. Golf columnist Dan Jenkins remarked,

"Tiger Woods on Sunday at the '97 Masters was the biggest lock in sports since Secretariat at the Belmont," alluding to that horse's shoe-in 1973 victory. In fact, the night before the tournament's final day, Colin Montgomerie announced to the other Masters contenders, "We're all human beings here, but there is no chance humanly possible that Tiger Woods is going to lose this golf tournament. No way . . . Faldo's not lying second, for a start, and Tiger Woods is not Greg Norman." Woods's putt on the last hole gave him an 18-under par total of 270, which broke the 72-hole record by one stroke, beating Jack Nicklaus's 1965 270 record, which had also been matched by Raymond Floyd in 1976.

Woods's Augusta victory came just two days before the 50th anniversary of the day Jackie Robinson broke the color barrier in professional baseball. When asked how he felt about being the first person of African-American heritage to win an event which until 1975 had permitted blacks on the course only as caddies, Woods remarked that Charlie Sifford, who was excluded from the Masters, and Lee Elder, the first black to play in the tournament, were the true pioneers.

"Because of them, I was able to play here," Woods said. "I was able to play on the PGA Tour. I was able to live my dream because of those guys. Lee came down here [to Augusta] and that just inspired me, and I knew what I had to do." Lee Elder, who drove to Augusta to watch Tiger win, was overcome by the young golfer's victory. "That's because I know how hard I had tried," Elder said, "and I knew how hard Charlie [Sifford] had tried and Pete Brown and Jim Dent and the rest [of the professional black golfers] had tried, and now this young man had done it on his first try."

The youngest person to ever win the Masters, Woods sparked a growing interest in golf among young people. "Everybody's talking about golf [now] and hopefully it's going to rub off on all the tours and players," said young LGPA champion Annika Sorenstam, remarking on the changes brought about by Tiger's appeal. According to Ira Ratner, director of the U.S. Junior Classic Golf Tour, the tournament circuit for juniors is so popular and fiercely competitive right now that "no matter how many tours [are added], there's not enough space for all the boys and girls who want to play."

The changing demographics of golf have become evident in the new lines of golf apparel designed for a younger generation. And for the first time ever, the USGA has slightly relaxed its rules regarding dress for golfing events. Just prior to the U.S. Open in June of 1997, the association announced that caddies would be allowed to wear shorts during games, provided they were tailored, Bermuda-length, and solid-colored. "It's about time they caught up with the times," said one caddie. "You look great in shorts and you're cool."

Tigermania helped to involve more young people in the sport. But the media attention did not seem to affect Woods. Arnold Palmer, whom Woods had sought out for advice, found that the young golfer was "very, very talented on the golf course and he handles himself very well off the golf course."

Byron Nelson, who watched Tiger play the 1997 Masters, remarked, "You couldn't teach Tiger's swing [but] there's nothing wrong with it. His balance is great; he never moves off the ball. His timing, his movement, his coordination are excellent. His swing is just one continuous motion."

*Four-time winner of the LGPA Player of the Year award, Nancy Lopez became only the fifth LGPA pro to exceed $1 million in career earnings. Lopez accomplished all of this with an unusual golf swing that many deemed faulty. "Her swing belongs to her and her alone," says veteran LPGA golfer Kathy Whitworth. "It's the same with Palmer and Nicklaus. Their swings aren't perfect, but look what they've done."*

Jack Nicklaus, who was paired with Woods at the 1996 U.S. Open, believed Tiger would win more of the coveted green Masters jackets than both he and Arnold Palmer put together. "I think he's phenomenal," said Nicklaus. "I don't think I had anywhere near the amount of media or public pressure that he's had, and he's handled it beautifully." As the old adage says, "the game of golf is 90% mental and 10% mental" and Tiger Woods showed that he could handle the pressure.

Tigermania followed Woods to the 1997 U.S. Open, which enjoyed its highest television ratings in ten years, due in part to speculation over whether Tiger might take the second leg of the Grand Slam. With all of the media hype surrounding the young Woods, many of Tiger's fans were surprised and disappointed when he did not win the June 1997 tournament. "I am human," Woods said, after 27-year-old Ernie Els of South Africa won the U.S. Open for the second time. "I wasn't born on some other planet. I think the way I won the Masters, people expected more from me." Golf commentators noted that the narrow fairways the USGA set on the course worked against Woods's long drives. Because it does not employ his distance advantage, the U.S. Open may prove the most difficult leg of the Grand Slam for Woods to win. But then, difficulty is the idea. As John Oswald, former chairman of an Open greens committee, said: "The Open is the greatest title there is. The course should be so hard, nobody can win it."

Despite his tie for 19th place at the U.S. Open, in June 1997 Woods became, for a time, the youngest player to lead the world golf rankings, temporarily moving Australia's Greg Norman down to second place. For those playing on the fiercely competitive PGA tour, Woods proved himself a dominant player, jolting other top players out of the catbird seat. His presence on the PGA tour made everyone work a little harder, which can only be good for the future of golf.

# CHRONOLOGY

| | |
|---|---|
| 1457 | James II of Scotland bans golf in the interest of national defense. |
| 1834 | William II confers title of royal and ancient upon golf club of St. Andrews. |
| 1848 | Introduction of the gutta percha ball. |
| 1861 | First British Open held; won by Old Tom Morris. |
| 1888 | Formation of first U.S. golf club, St. Andrew's at Yonkers, New York. |
| 1894 | USGA formed. |
| 1901 | Rubber-cored golf ball is invented. |
| 1913 | 21-year-old Francis Ouimet defeats Vardon and Ray in the U.S. Open, popularizing golf in America. |
| 1921 | St. Andrews introduces first limitation on size and weight of golf balls. |
| 1922 | Americans win the first Walker Cup match with Great Britain. |
| 1927 | U.S. team defeats Britain in inaugural Ryder Cup match. |
| 1930 | Bobby Jones scores a grand slam, winning the U.S. and British Opens and Amateurs in the same year. |
| 1932 | Augusta National Golf Club, designed by Bobby Jones and Alistar Mackenzie, opens. |
| | USGA approves the 1.68 inch diameter golf ball, making it the standard. |
| | First Curtis Cup match for women is held. |
| 1938 | USGA limits the number of clubs a player may use to fourteen. |
| 1945 | Byron Nelson wins a record eleven consecutive events. |
| 1949 | LPGA formed. |
| 1953 | First nationally televised golf tournament. |
| 1963 | Arnold Palmer becomes first golfer to win over $100,000 in one year. |
| | Jack Nicklaus wins his first Masters, and for 17 years holds record of being youngest person to do so. |
| 1971 | Alan Shepard hits a six-iron shot from the surface of the moon. |
| 1975 | Lee Elder becomes first African American invited to play at the Masters. |
| 1986 | Jack Nicklaus wins his sixth Masters; at age 46 he becomes the oldest player to win the Masters. |
| 1990 | Fanny Sunesson, hired by Nick Faldo, becomes the PGA tour's first full-time female caddie. |
| 1997 | 21-year-old Tiger Woods becomes youngest to win the Masters Tournament; Woods sets a Masters record of 270. |

# GOLF RECORDS

## MEN'S

### THE MASTERS

Most wins: Jack Nicklaus, six times, (1963, 1965–66, 1972, 1975, 1986)

Consecutive wins: Jack Nicklaus (1965–66) and Nick Faldo (1989–90)

Lowest 18-hole total: 63, Nick Price of Zimbabwe, 1986

Lowest 72-hole total: 270, Tiger Woods, 1997

### THE U.S. OPEN

Most wins: Four players have won the title four times: Willie Anderson (1901, 1903–5), Bobby Jones (1923, 1926, 1929–30), Ben Hogan (1948, 1950–1, 1953), Jack Nicklaus (1962, 1967, 1972, 1980)

Most consecutive wins: Three, Willie Anderson (1903–05)

Lowest 18-hole total: 63, three players: Johnny Miller (1973), Jack Nicklaus and Tom Weiskopf (1980)

Lowest 72-hole total: 272, Jack Nicklaus (1980) and Lee Janzen (1993)

### THE BRITISH OPEN

Most wins: Harry Vardon, six times, (1896, 1898–99, 1903, 1911, 1914)

Most consecutive wins: Four, by Tom Morris Jr. (1868–70, 1872; event not held in 1871)

Lowest 72-hole total: 267 by Greg Norman (1993)

### THE PGA CHAMPIONSHIP

Most wins: two players have won the title five times: Walter Hagen (1921, 1924–27) and Jack Nicklaus (1963, 1971, 1973, 1975, 1980)

Lowest 72-hole total: 271, Bobby Nichols (1964)

## WOMEN'S

### THE U.S. OPEN (SINCE 1946)

Most wins: Two players have won the title four times: Betsy Rawls (1951, 1953, 1957, 1960) and Mickey Wright (1958–59, 1961, 1964)

Most consecutive wins: Two, by five players: Mickey Wright (1958–59), Donna Caponi (1969–70), Susie Berning (1972–73), Hollis Stacey (1977–78), and Betsy King (1989–90)

Lowest 72-hole total: 277, by Liselotte Neumann of Sweden, 1988

### LPGA CHAMPIONSHIP (SINCE 1955)

Most wins: Mickey Wright, four times (1958, 1960–61, 1963)

Lowest 72-hole total: 267, by Betsy King (1992)

### NABISCO DINAH SHORE (SINCE 1972)

Most wins: Amy Alcott, three times (1983, 1988, 1991)

Lowest 72-hole total: 273, Amy Alcott (1991)

### DU MAURIER CLASSIC (SINCE 1973)

Most wins: Pat Bradley, three times, (1980, 1985–86)

Lowest 72-hole total: 276, by three players: Pat Bradley and Ayako Okamoto (1986) and Cathy Johnston (1990)

# FURTHER READING

Barkow, Al. *History of the PGA Tours*. New York: Doubleday, 1989.

Italia, Robert. *100 Unforgettable Moments in Pro Golf*. Minneapolis: Abdou & Daughters, 1996.

Peper, George et al. *Golf in America: The First One Hundred Years*. New York: Harry N. Abrams, Inc., 1988.

Wind, Herbert W. *The Story of American Golf*. Stamford, CT: Classics Golf, 1994.

# INDEX

**PICTURE CREDITS** AP/Wide World Photos: pp. 6, 60; Boston Public Library Print Department: pp. 10, 21, 22, 24, 29, 31, 39, 42; Corbis-Bettmann: pp. 12, 38; UPI/Corbis-Bettmann: pp. 18, 40, 57; Old Chicago Golf Shop: pp. 16, 17; Library of Congress: p. 2; National Archives: pp. 32, 33, 36; Reuters/Corbis-Bettmann: pp. 44, 51, 53; UPI: p. 46

**MARY E. HULL** received her B.A. in history from Brown University in 1995. She is a freelance writer based in Boston, where she writes for educational publishers and businesses. In 1997 the New York Public Library Association selected Ms. Hull's book *Struggle and Love* as one of the best books of the year for teenagers.